GLITCHWORK

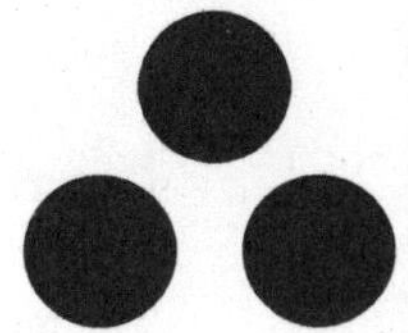

MANTRA MUKIM

Published 2026 by the87press
The 87 Press C.I.C.
87 Stonecot Hill
Sutton
Surrey
SM3 9HJ
www.the87press.co.uk

ISBN: 978-1-0684880-2-3

Printed and bound by CPI Group (UK) Ltd, Croydon, CR0 4YY

Cover image: Nasreen Mohamedi, *Untitled*
Courtesy: Masanori Fukuoka, Glenbarra Collection

Design: Stanislava Stoilova [www.sdesign.graphics]

Typeset in Arizona by s-design.

Arizona is a custom font designed by Elias Hanszer and produced by Dinamo

EU GPSR Authorised Representative
LOGOS EUROPE, 9 rue Nicolas Poussin, 17000, LA ROCHELLE, France
E-mail: Contact@logoseurope.eu

for radial lines

for my father

Contents

1   ~~Plant~~

5   **Raipur**

25   ~~Plant~~

29   **Glitchwork**

67   ~~Plant~~

71   **With Sur**

100   ~~Plant~~

101   **Notes**

████████████████████████████████████ the plant is estimated to
be about one year behind schedule████████████████████████████████
██

The plant ███████ is to have an initial capacity ███████████

plant

refused by the privately owned

plant

I. RAIPUR

and twisting   the washed
cloth of sky   over the stilts

egrets return
having picked locusts

from the backs of buffaloes
all morning   an amber gap dries out

the washed cloth of sky   echoes from a
single note   tricks of skin   see the repetition

of water   as rain   the escarpment in chitrakut
is 'one thick fold on the earth's fabric'   built

to hold a tune   breath tickling   the washed cloth
of sky   when i say *ambient*   i say tamarind

ripening in record time   ambient hand
stroking last night's   dough   in fridge light

wind deep in the belly of the factory   blowing iron ore
into the sore ears   of the house   a lazy eyed man

somewhere in kondagaon   firms up bronze
armies   with muzzles poking   the washed cloth of sky

hand is full   wading searching
the edge of summer   is there a rose

beyond the rice fields   a birthmark
hovers above the neighbourhood   etched

in bauxite dust   boys behind takeaways
rework playlists   as the plant destroys us

but my hand is full   of words   like
grass   perforating the old lattice

leave your eggs here   in the helix of my ear
safe   in the 'world-class banking scheme'

raipur is where the earth's warmth is hatched

this hand is full   of other hands   colours
cracking the dense world   distorting the

clearing   when i say clearing   i say maoists
at the bus stop   saying yes   to the hill myna

clearing the thick august morning   pulling out
old samples and hits   as the 'export-quality'

teak wood around it shivers   tired &
often leaving   but at least the hand is full

my song says no   keeping a secret that changes clouds
in a grove of scared   interfaith lovers   scattering the message

of haze   day's first light   wedged in a spider's web   the house
has four hands   one of which is always repairing   another

rattling on the roof   offers gifts   to passing sparrows
a flatbed truck   transporting loudspeakers to a political rally

crosses the street   blasting from it   my song says no   bamboo
scaffolds   tearing construction tarps   like piercings on

cows   the tailor who won the urdu academy   poetry award
lets neighbours   loiter in his shop   as he sews

a new button   on my school shirt   swarm of mosquitoes
cover yesterday's dead mango seed   in a wetdream

of extraction   to the surplus time   my song says no
the devotee looks up   & cuts the river with a coin

a small surcharge   for raipur's slowness   where a new
coal block   cannot die within the land   & dusk crude

as cash   circulates in the skies raiding   softening
the first-person lyric blow   my song says no

the day of my return is a day   moving across the page
a face without tricks   a stack of grain   lumpen sun

stitching roof to roof   eye seeks
the fruits of deviation   overturned truck

near the toll plaza   a ginger afloat before defeat
a public nose   the debris   of forgotten houses

hovering below   three fighter planes   doors tousled
from six directions   the day of my return is a day

i pluck a mahua leaf   with its petiole intact
from the edge of abhuj-mar   its loneliness

in my hands   concertina wire   at the edge
of a rice field   a sliver of flesh   hiding

in the film   dims the frame   the harvest
full of now   settles down   the day

of my return   a day   low clouds pass
a message   to the clipped marigolds   time

cuts through water   my return   shamed
for its deferral   the day of my return is a day

fill the eye   with slow hyphae
neighbour's tree   breaking the border

with thousand hyphens   on its tip   & sitafal
the unrealisable dream   of revolution

fruit   in present tense   moving
the ghost suburbs   fill the eye

with risky collectives   index finger   dragging
the screen to moisture   inscription   not touch

of the new fascist calendar   smoke in the hormones
iron in the bush   shape: the prosthetic of land

fill the eye   with mongrel archives
catbirths   in abandoned   chariots

yes   the debris yes the structure   a stowaway
word   in the lung   surfaces   at the sight

of the machine   guts open   daring
a sentence   fill the eye   with tragic repair

dust again   moving   hushing the land
mouths of sal trees   agape at dusk   spit crows

the lake i saw   from the car window   goes by the name:
gap   the temple with seven pillars   floating on the banks

is a pasture   men bending over it   known as:
error   chewing tobacco   rinsing mouths

with lake water   dust again   covers the bronzes
covers the welded image of the eye   the ancient threshold

of the forest   where a noise once heard   foams
airs   without decay   among the crops

of water chestnut   half immersed   half in debt   the farmer
dizzy   pulling out from the marsh   into the air   his first

harvest   rubbing raipur   with dust again   the archaeological
dig   calls the earth: a witness   to its true shape

once a factory shed   the excavation site at sirpur   reveals a face
the very machine   at the centre of history   an ancient buddha

in bhumisparsha mudra   with a shrivelled grove looming
behind him   the tour guide   jumped the walls of the dig

as a kid   to hear the heavy breath   escaping the ripped
flesh of his village floor   he pinched the day   till it was dust again

lifting the mirrors of libgen   eye finds its new
non-cached form   elevated pilasters   firmly

masoned   estate walls   now open like
paddy fields   snatched from their stem   the root

of receiving   recessed drafts of raipur   surface
against the finality   of form   in the mirrors of libgen

land becomes easy   for the open sourced   sky
forges sky   sleep mimics sleep   i sit crosslegged

anchored to the pirate   spit of land   pitching
analogue hasps   in the wired drift   of the sacred

'rinsework is downloading'   niyogi in the union
niyogi in the dialect   departure of homesick

swallows   falling diagonally falling fast   through
the mirrors of libgen   a peepal emerges   caressing

gashing   the temple wall   the structural pus
of private property   evening with all its arteries

unfolds 'rinsework is passage' i find a trick within
my shoulder   carrying   the mirrors of libgen

grass like tension   there is a no   from the long
lost land   uttered while parting   use it   to refuse tax-

onomy   to get away   from the cold centre
of the forest   speech collects debt   the letter

not yet here   a fierce no   among the endless
crowds of yes   hyphenated at the very site

the fruit is eaten   above its mellow core   yes
a mole in the hq of refusal   envying the ever

throbbing   no   no is a shoreline   a capacity
with zero kills   turning away from the beast

having studied its movement   for far too long
no   will urge the sky   to give up its claim   on us

a fold   in the lake   disperses the night
three birds are quiet   within me

shivering   with the dull ache   of suburbia
the eyes sinking   in the image of error   i

turn to the edicts   condemning salt   for weakness
disperses the night   the edge of raipur   explodes

with ayurvedic scams   we enter   the agnostic
dream   of a deity   in a blast furnace

monks   in gloves   caress smelt iron sheets
flattened marrow   of yearning   disperses

the night   apparitions   in the gridlock
in the planner's notes   rewires the local   god

suspended   above the mall   muscular tableaux
from ramayana   epic grift   disperses the night

descent of the crossfade in the grotto
descent of construction in the song
descent of the sublime in the gridline
descent of gentleness in the map
descent of thresholds in the forest
descent of friendship in the promise
descent of solar bird in the sanctuary
descent of language in the muscle
descent of violence in the elbow
descent of the step in the book
descent of breath in the steel
descent of glitch in the face
descent of myth in the oil
descent of limit in the gift
descent of caste in the fire
descent of form in militancy
descent of soul in the face
descent of spit in the money
descent of sly in the sky

isotropic caverns in the trees rise   expectant mongrels
wade   through spring   chasing the song

sensing a tremble   in the line   skaters await
the earth   heroes await   peripheries

frugal affects in the trees rise   measured
hills stop blooming   fixing an exploding   skin

cavalcades flattened   on the forest floor
pass through   clay   not yet raipur

the ancient day with a hole   in its cranium
collapses in the tunnel   soft detritus

in the trees rise   rice has been their
threshold   never their door   into the body

cutting through   the gleaner's shadow
radical boredom   in the trees rise

he pulled me aside   to the ancient threshold
of the house   where a teak forest   once operated

as the final moat   standing before the pastoral   i was
told: you came from a low storm   planted   above raipur

bringing hail   in the temple   & taking down
your uncle's new hyundai santro   you came from .rar

extension   compressed as an eight-bit angel   a vagrant
download   in your cousin's cybercafé   swastika melting

over the tubes   you came from a righteous vagueness
that conceals   the soft tissue   of the grid

strangeness of steel   burrowed in   your father's palm
a loud hustle   you came with a chhatim leaf

stuck to your heart   that had to be surgically extracted
sowed   nurtured at the façade   of the house   where cows

seek love   the broken middle   of bhimpalasi
you came from asking — if history is a singalong

metal's endless duration   its fibrous snail-cut flakes
tempered joints   in fingers   softened by gleaning

jungles leaking   through stitch-wires   toes tight
in rivulets of scrap   flint's common sense

an angel   leaving   an angel   welding wire
incidents of colour   in the half-sky   a hoarder's

warning   conjunctions   will not redeem us
thereness   hereness   an alphabet's foreskin

between   the glove and the finger   spread the grease
on autotelic mornings   on hatred's breath

animating the thing   lost below   the lines of the tragic
grid   the unruly grid   now melted into hours

but the interface   red-vented bulbul's
housing crisis   nesting subprime in the shed

'metal brings no owners   only settlers'   friends loved
me once   for all the trees   i could name in bilaspur

counterfeits   accompany the fire   welding
melding   carrying the face   to subtle

constructions   broken limbs of words
will heal once again   mouths will nest   there

here   a cross section   in the pond
the last hour   of shedding   this catatonic thread

weightless   plaiting   barely leaves the game
metadata slipping   away into the dusk

without any challenge   family of three   an election
booth in a soybean field   vote wrecking the nail

all images   of foreigners   falling short of foreignness
not just in the mesh   but our there   here

edge   of a medieval rampart   an empty
rusting cannon   i press my ears   against its open

mouth   and listen   inside this combative edge
for a vacant sound   without spar

like six steel fingers   lacking
arteries   a chord   in the afterglow

outside this edge   nations are solutions
to writing   spring   stalls the book

inside it   a raging debt   glance shaped
quiet   i drop a few words   in the barrel:

'formulae' 'afternoon' 'cornice' 'tally'

words once used   as signals   committed
to degrowth   in this barrel a cessation of flows

i press the edge   of the cannon   for hours
until i hear your voice   thawing inside

a great but trembling scaffold   we carry
our neighbours' property within us   eclogues

in the shape   of kiln   construction of the house
in a series of sixteen hundred   tragic events

nodes that tether the structure   to the vacant plot
the rise of the plant   through the floor plan

in the cement   an index   of first lines
in the material   a dormant volume

what makes the columns   of the book   touch
urdhavaloka   a great   but trembling prosody

                — we carry beginnings

impossible sky >   those who are capable of shouting
in civil lines   do not need the grid to protect them

local sky >   a face lessening at dussehra   plunge of the body
in the stanza   known as the room   that quivers

rice sky >   speaking only half a word   why
must the ink be preserved when the grain is diffused

stuck sky >   bury the book among landmines   that foretell
a forest   raipur celebrates gravity   as it dissipates

failed sky >   jain heaven is an empty place   our realm
is here   jain hell is a non-place   our perfection is here

sponge iron sky >   light   clutches the ankle   the navel
of the woman selling gourd   mesh is lilt   as addition

autochthonous sky >   grim diagnosis   by a siraha in sarguja
is sorcery ever   like the poem   embarrassed of itself

sky's sky >   like writer's writer   is a business without
calculation   a tissue of quotes   it offers chance   a chance

raipur is less than north   raipur is less than west
grammatical rift   raipur is less than a
debt   raipur is less than the torso of
the meridian of bastar   raipur is less
less than the eight stomachs of a gaur
local goddess raipur is less than the 3rd
than the azimuth of hawala cash raipur
raipur is less than grid-induced trauma
raipur is less than the thirteenth smoke
crows   raipur is less than   the totalised

raipur is less than the width of a pseudo
bifold   raipur is less than a friendly
mahant ghasidas   raipur is less than
than the diagram of the soul   raipur
raipur is less   than the six arms of a
surrealist manifesto   raipur is less
is less than loops   in a surdas hymn
raipur is less than   the 7th fragment
raipur is less than   seven prolific
plant   raipur is less than   four crpf

officers   raipur is less than its own concept raipur is less than east raipur is less than south

refused by the Soviets ███████████████ the ██████████████████████
plant ██

██ the plant is estimated ██

██

██████ satisfactorily.

700 Indians are to be trained in

the plant

plant and

plant

amounting to Govern-

ment

II. GLITCHWORK

The book is a psychogeographic account of opacity. The book is an architectonic account of the ocular. It narrates the difference between darshan and gaze, explaining why one suits the fiend and the other the cinematographer. Darshan, this book notes, is derived from the Sanskrit word darshana meaning sight, vision, or appearance, and passes through a lineage of sacral demotic to be now referred to specific instances of visibility, of being granted vision to something rare, holy, or supernatural in tangible form. The book cites numerous instances where a forlorn lover, a mechanical tool, or a bureaucratic occurrence has been made visible, or rather offered a vision of themselves, through this otherwise sacral mode of access. For the book darshan is not gazing, it does not start in the eye, but in the face of the other that gives the eye a chance, a lucky break. Gaze is direct, piercing, critical. Gaze extends the hegemony of eye, darshan, the hegemony of the seen. The book spends all its thirteen hundred pages tracking the loose meridian between darshan and gaze. The book is how our feud with the senses first began.

Tala's hair is bound by snake coils forming a turban over his head, he is a local god, a domestic biome. Two snake hoods pop over his shoulders with urgency. They look on from either side of his head. A lizard forms his nose and its hind legs curve beneath it and make the eyebrows. His eyes are formed, deformed, in the image of a frog's, plump and wide, to navigate the grid, in all its apertures. His moustache is two pieces of stone made to resemble the shiny yet serrated outer skin of an unidentifiable fish, while a crab sits over his lower lip and chin, completing the face. This face acts as the central node for all the faces in the region. The face on which other faces perch. Face not as itself, but as a catalogue of every other possible face. Tala's tongue is hidden inside his mouth. No one quite knows which creature gives it shape, or who speaks through it. Two peacocks with their oversized tails hanging above them create the ears, while the sea-creatures, makaras, with mouth agape sit on the two shoulders out of which his arms hang down towards his torso. Tala's fingernails are upright, while his hands point towards the viewer, in a gesture neither accusatory nor amicable. It is a hand tied firmly to the body. Even in its peripheral position away from the face, its firm and resigned stance diverts attention back to the face. A thin snake, unrelated to the plump reptile coiled over Tala's head, circles his waist like a firm belt. A rotund belly swings over it. Two human faces are embedded over Tala's chest, covering his nipples, and one zoned out human face stretches all over his stomach. His penis, erect and grazing against his bulbous belly, is the head of a tortoise, caught peering outside its shell. His testicles are two cowbells. The bells have concave lips and miniscule clappers that are firmly stuck to the thighs. His metallic testicles, a prosthetic of echoing libido, bring together the iron mined from the ground beneath and the future of the manifold face. Adjacent to the bells, four human faces stare back from Tala's thighs. Two in the front, facing us, and two on either side. The faces above his knees are perhaps attached to bodies in genuflection, as they are accompanied by a pair of hands joined in prayer. Their invisible bodies bent inside the grid, looking out. These two faces on Tala's body are the only ones without moustaches. Right below these faces, instead of what would have been Tala's kneecaps, there are two subdued faces of the lion. Going by their cropped hair and prominent nose, it is clear that Tala has never looked a lion in the face. In fact, his kneecaps might have been a weak invitation for the face of the lion to finally arrive in the grid. No one in this district has any idea why Tala carries the faces he does, or if there is a secret to their arrangement. One ruling speculation points to the zodiac symbology: Tala's body representing a form of a zodiac-circle with all the iconic animals present. Others have traced in the one sundry face the animals that serve as taxis, vahanas, to gods themselves and have seen Tala himself as a vehicle, or an index of divine vehicular technology. Despite his stature, Tala is not considered a major deity but a subsidiary one. He is placed outside the gate on the left, as an attendant figure against the crenelated wall, guarding and parting the way to the central face of the temple. The valley that surrounds Tala has two braided rivers running through it with lateral channel movements. It has given rise to several small mud islands that surface during low tides. On those islands one can sometimes spot a crow with a face almost entirely its own.

dusk hides the hand from work   it leads the hand away   from what is precarious
from objects sovereign and inviolate away from songs already built to teach the
hand   how to hold suffering   make earth into its other through planning
perching   along the precinct   waiting   dusk presses the hand against a stone
draws a thick line around it   the early palaeolithic theory of difference: between
touch   and labour   intimacy   and impression the hand holds more air   than
air   it retreats from the stone   fists closed conspiring with dusk   to leave the day
without day   leave work   without work   in dusk no hand moves   none breathe
and fissure   none bleed materials   for alienation is arrangement of what briefly
glows against what perennially gathers: a spear mute inside the animal   a hollow
within a line   dusk is concrete   not form   dusk hides the hand from work

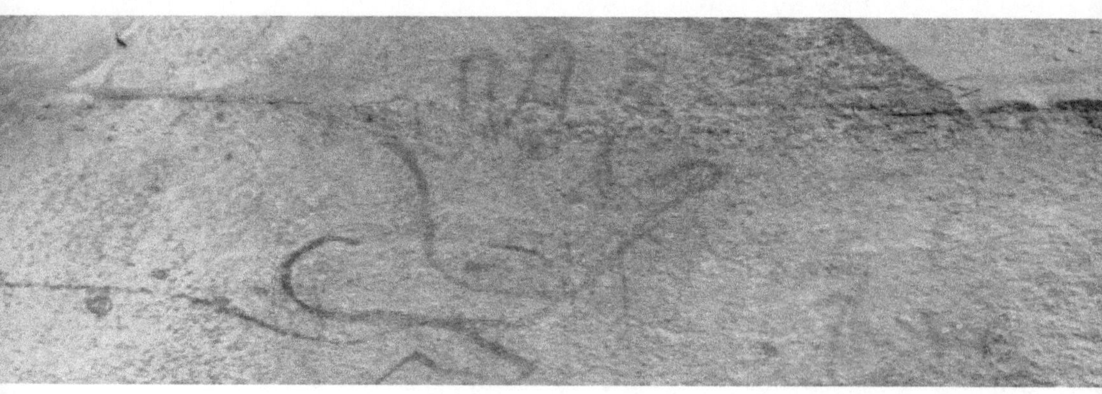

in wong may's game   changing translations of the tang poets   i come
across yuan zhen's short poem 'reply to a friend who dreamt of me'
barely a day after   a friend   texts me   in the early hours   saying   he has
had a dream of me   and it terrorises me   to enter his dream   without
leaving myself   without leaving myself there   my reply is giddy   having
learnt   having been   elsewhere somewhere   not here   away from here
& again to leave   zhen's reply   a reply poetics   not—for the dream   not—
to reply with a dream   but with the day   my day as a reply   in reply to
his dream of me   full of me   i give him   my day   a reply from me   from
the newly inaugurated outskirts   of raipur   my day   trapped in the faux
grids   of a ghotul exhibit   codpiece swaying over the commons flux of
ink   still visible   in my day purged lines   concaves converging   harvest
rituals reimagined for   liberal subtopias   my day   has never dreamt   of
friends   the long hand   of friends' dream of me   presses against the eye
covering my friend's dream of me   as his friend   my reply   is a dream
of friendship   without the friend in it   dream of my day   replying to this
friend   replying to the dream of me   but not as a friend   as a reply   that
i reply to him   not to him as my friend   but as one who   has had a dream
of me   without me   my reply is me   asking my friend's dream of me
for a reply to my dream   the dream of sitting at the mouth of the river
staring into the dream where our raw muscle convulses eternally in his left
handed   day

— sorry but i could not help noticing how your thyroid gland is shaped like a house sparrow   moving without movement   dull tired yet in constant inertia   maybe a glitch or two inherited from the old masters in our weakness a hormone often abandons its fealty the firefly abandons the fire i can tell in immunity   all waiting is an intense bioform   immunity animates the gaze towards the lines of the hill it gets tired of standing erect against the bailadila hills & falls on the surface of the book it lies under the plant eating soil splintered by the wind when i see your gland for too long i see the frontier valley a stillborn voice without timber sinking under the deccan stone it has a singular weave your gland have you noticed how it looks like the hump of an ox the autoimmune organ contracting revolting at the first hint of the universal does it not always move against its own through air through song you know margery kempe would have loved raipur for how it stages that evangelical praxis how it collapses like a text but baits like a deity how its metal is immunity much like your gland it schemes against itself to fear to oil to set off the holy grid —

~

[अदानी वापस जाओ]

in small shifts   air brings between their toes the bauxite of history in

big shifts   they pull the sky   & press it down on tectonic faults   of the

present   in long shifts they churn out clouds   that take our sorrows to

the local gods & leave them covered in soot   in slow shifts they discard

this poem in a valley so deep   warblers   nest among its lines   spending

monsoon in night shifts they bury their dead   extract from the living the

debris of light   in a tight shift they put fire   to what is left of slowness

in overtime shift they rewrite the alphabet   based on value   in the rice-

fuelled noon shift   they turn into amber & glow all the way to raipur   in

final shift   they leave their hands   someplace where   they will be found

      & used   to lift the land again —

let us not lift the land again   its wide rivulets   its central longings   let us not shame it with all the covert names   for the grid   gash it with estimates   heal it with measure   corners of this land   stretch all the way   where lessness has no meaning   gaze has no gifts   the wonder that was promised   by dandkaranya's many questions   is not to be found beneath it   our fingers in the gloves   our iron in the sleeves   of the earth covering our voice   is the unbroken membrane shed by strophes   let us fall on falling   rest on our backs   ask   why is there   so little sun in our arms   why is the night   fungible   why should they   never return in the small hours   the eye loses its myth   & the landscape turns around what it cannot name   in the long hours   a stalk of champa becomes common stock   & offer its secrets   to the rice field   in the zero hours   the long dead chimney   of the soviet-made steel plant   has its lichen harvested for water   by a family of sparrows   in the long hours   the labour of calm   brings back to the body   all it has lost & will lose   to the supply chain   in the prime hours   the voice is asked to redeem   the oil buried in the stone   & the song not

yet ours

everywhere the book   a revenge of the invisible   on the visible

in the teeth of demolition   in the toes of the nation   seedily stationed in

the wings of the cormorant   drying itself across a bark   in the special

economic zone   within the sacerdotal vehicle   abandoned in the parking

its windscreen choking with proselytizing print of a vernacular crusade in

the syndrome of the mantralaya   under a file   marked tender applications

for special fibre gloves   employed the meteorite destruction unit   in the

industrial solution to writing   in the rally to purge   rally to reinstate the

acropodium for that bipedal angel   in the cold war archive in the catalogues

of steel production   in the central plateaus   registered   through the tepid

ink of intelligence   in the line that can only command   but not commence

in the noise of the document   in the weft of the metal   in my father's face

at fifty   with the old custom lines   going through raipur cassette house

in the medieval hagiography of liberation   a cosmic map with eight climes

and four rewards   in my uncle's hardware store   behind the wet wall of

storage through a blunt brick   in the blow room of the obsolescent rice mill

in the centre of ink's calamitous impulse   in the new topological model

where   the dimension of the book is

'no one will ever nuke raipur'

A war on meteorology is coming   make it new suburban
industrially sublime   virally ambient   cloudier over the jungle with
syncopated loops   less sharp less local   slow forested   tremblingly finite
digitally rose   centrally arranged   fished from the downstream   outside
the hygiene   of the optical   expressing density in the cool of the grid
expressing the shimmer   when trapped in the fronds of salphi   make
it watery   like solid ideogram melting on the welding gloves   feverish
like angels   carefully taking apart the government of the world   make it
the book   as the practice of sahaja   make it   the book as our wreckage

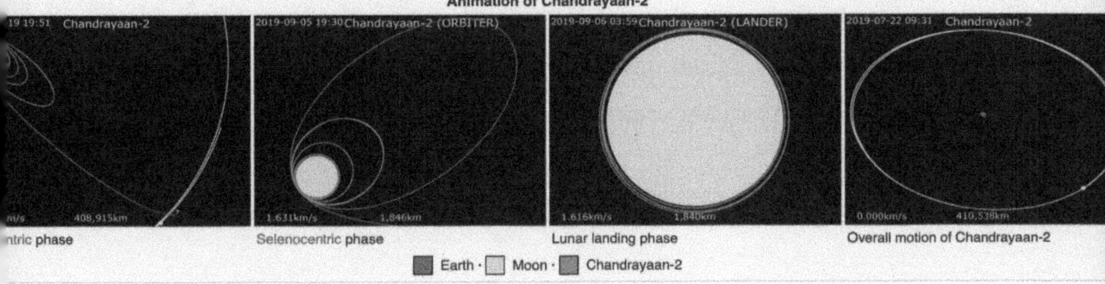

Chandrayan-2 still circles the moon, reaching once every week the precise traumatic point from where it dropped the lander on 6 September 2019. On the day the lander plummeted into the gravitational well alone, slowly glitching from within, unknown to the knots appearing on my hand as I tracked its descent with an epistolary desire — a word addressed to the bottom of the well, a surface that itself remains unbroken to be able to contain, to receive. The book does not draw water without a sacrifice. A peril unknown to the sovereign watching the lander from Sriharikota, a glitch is a fall not a landing. Did we think landing was belonging? The lander was scheduled to land softly on the Moon surface at 20:23 UTC, soft not because it wished to null all difference between itself and the crystallised feldspar, submerging itself in a vast sameness. Instead, in this dream of landing softly the lander was to sneak around the various crevices of its host without sticking out, like a termite sheltering in the spine of the book. Landing softly in this circumstance, without breaking the skin of the Moon or its own skin, would have meant being allowed into the land as land, tilling of soil with soil, not as contesting but as constellating desires. The prime landing site (PLS54) chosen for the Chandrayan-2 was at 70.90267°S 22.78110°E, 600 kilometre from the South Pole, a coordinate now trapped inside the machine's algid mouth as its last word. On the high plain between the craters Manzinus C and Simpelius N, where now the lander's debris spreads for at least seven kilometres, there are unmarked graves for every little organ that travelled under a single body from the edge of dusk, glistening with metals skinned from Dandkaranya. On a slow buffering telecast I see the lander abandon its axis and relinquish all contact. The ruin is a scaffold until it is a ruin. The Failure Analysis Committee blames a software glitch in the lander that caused it to crash at a high velocity and fail to land softly.

Glitch is a wound without an outside. It is not the book. It owes us nothing.

beauty is not the home you think it is

Why is S and Sh so intricate to the history of violence? Mother could not say the velar fricative 'Sh' when I was born. I was named with a different, a more diabolical, fricative. Soon I learnt that in Assam, at the height of the Assam Agitation from 1979 to 1985, people were publicly made to count from 1 to 7 to decide if they were Assamese or illegal Bengali migrants. In Assamese the number is 7 is pronounced [Xat] with a velar fricative [X], while in Bangla the number is pronounced [SAT], close to its Hindi iteration. A criminalised velar limit of the mother tongue? A shrine of gentleness in the body? Plucking the rinds of light getting away from the lattice, I say Sh followed by Sa followed by Sh. 'Shibboleth is not what kills us, it is the terror, the error, our sacrifices to beauty'. A turbulent airflow in the mouth is when the grid identifies its trespassers from its devotees. Speech is not itself the glitch, it is not the end, it is not even the extraordinary coagulate touching, revamping the mesh as it leaves.

~

Today I learnt to ask myself: how can one receive the edge of land   Is it sensible to go to this edge, the edge of the only land one knows   Who prospers by the edge, who is banished there   Edge as the end of archives   Edge as a movement away from the centre but not towards the banlieue towards displacement itself   Is there anything truly beyond the edge   Or just more of the same—more of the limit   Can this limit be a line that animates the land   that ferments trouble in the archive returns miscellany to miscellany   Can it produce a blueprint on how to move among objects that do not belong   Can it wrinkle

Today I learnt to ask myself: how can one receive vastness   not as vastness but as a radial membrane   a line   Is there a vastness that lives among us without accident   I have two languages   neither mine   neither capable of conducting vastness as anything   except vastness   comrades in a monopoly Can one give up measure without emulating vastness itself   They ask: is the book vast enough   Is the grid not too vast for its own good   In the tier-two city   all desire is displacement   every open site a failing   Is it not vastness that offers the forest   to the forest   the line   to the line

Line is a movement on earth, neither away nor within. It has no explicit intention of turning into a tyrant if it comes to power. There are lines all over a kuccha ghar. The clay solidifies and cracks around its folds. A pukka ghar has sharper and fewer lines running on its edges, announcing the frontiers of the house. The ripening of the house is a management of lines. Line is flatness. Line is a body with a glitch interred in its appendix. A body has all the lines it can have. Line is the failure of love leading to justice. A space without width is line. The next spiritual hoax is a line. Line is a segment without sex. Line is the humid aftermath of the camera. One does not go to the line to stay but to practise awaiting. What is it that moves the line towards the vacuity—never towards itself—where does it find the resources to not make its beginnings and ends a scandal. Line is without nature, but also heroically without a grid. Line does not fold back in line, like dough. Line resists passion, passio, patior or suffering, which comes with being part of any deal. All iconicity is the bane of the line. The cunning of the line is its greatest attribute. Line is border. Line is flutter. It accompanies the stretched fabric drying across seven floors below grandmother's window. Line quarries the sky, quarries the machine. It quarries   the face.

Each line is born with three hands that it uses to wage a war against sensory reductionism. Some lines are born with a non-terrestrial vision. Few lines I have known personally were born either as too much or as too little. There are still lines out there waiting to be added to the endless mesh. Plainer surfaces with concentrated depths — 'each line is born of effort, history and pain'. The book is full of lines that do not intersect nor give us a mesh. The book reeks of the hand. One line alone can birth a swarm; it can bring voice to the world. A line born out of wedlock is generally rewarded with depth. Lines born in raipur have severe back pain. They do not know their source, they often let the calamity shape

them

Belonging has never been an issue with the line. It has been through so much. It readily gathers. It finds tangential exits. Line has the simplicity of its mass. Line sits on the ground as its own construction. It is responsible for its own circuit. Is the world really more available to the line? What can line do that the world can-not? Line has lived through intense compression of urban plurality. It has the defeat of polyhedral structures written all over it. Line moves in the factory as waste—it moves in the plant as artifice. A line can be bent only so far before it stops its work. The work of the line is departure. Line is all for people, but also for post-populations. A community of lines is never gated. They have been try-ing to draw an outline of Buddha's posture. What is the weight of this line? Line inherits violence from a bulldozer, horizon from the forest. For some its uneven-ness is holy. Line splits your paan leaf in two. It lets a shop inhabit the nave of a plant. Line clears its dues by resting on its back.

the   long   poem   is   the   carapace   of   the   world

In his essay 'The End of A Long Poem', Gajanan Madhav Muktibodh decries the long poem, a form he perfected over his short career, for its 'terrifying protruding quality'. He knows that the long poem is not a drilling machine, it is not to be used to pierce the earth's surface, it is not to burrow under the skin and uncover an original shell. There is no original shell. The terrifying duration of Muktibodh's long poem is not committed to discovery, but to the swerve. Muktibodh is terrified of measuring the poem, of scaling the line. For what it might become if it is made to actually fit its object. The world loathes the cover of a long poem. It is not a cover full of accretion. Nor a cover for concealment. Long poem spreads the message of breakdown in the four known directions. Muktibodh's old house in Rajnandgaon is a state-run museum full of dull curiosities. The staircase in the house, a fixture in his long poems, has the subject ascending and descending around a line. A landscape without scarcity. Everything one sees in the house, through its many windows, protrudes further, lingers longer, than it should. Duration is how grids die.

i used the river to witness something | maybe a point | where first | or firstness
| splits open lateness | enacts a delay of origins | a leaking grid | and in all
this a dot of shrunken space | a small measure of dirt collapsing on itself |
sending fissures through the biome | offering a river| buried deep within its
own skin | carrying no memories | but just a name: udgam or source | a name
as a deity painted on the town wall | a place is a deity when it is emptied of
time | as we hiked down an old shepherd's path overlooking the parish church
of warwickshire a friend once said to me: 'the great sausage of time is the
same everywhere, cut it where you like' | sameness is what brings the source
of narmada a name, water as water, even at its very beginning, at its radix, no
rupture | itself all the way through, a sameness that delivers a name | & to bear
that sameness as a ritual |a diminutive elephant in stone sits near the source
pond | with a queue of pilgrims contorting themselves to crawl underneath
its belly and emerge on the other side to re-enact the myth that all rivers
are born after ducking the event of oppression | through sheer passage

'a *linear* geographic feature with only one mouth and one source' | freedom
draws from sameness | protected in amarkantak behind a bulletproof
plexiglass | on four sides of the actual source, the alleged mouth of
narmada | a dot clogged with threads around it, like the centre of a fruit—
null but providing | in the compound the only thing consecrated is this
origin | a lush delay | at which rose petals are thrown hitting the glass
box and becoming buoyant in the pond around the source | a reification
of movement| a site where one is allowed only bare feet | to encounter

the river as a biological fact| a body with organs| more vulnerable to
feet other than its own| mother to some| narmada meanders through its
errata —

Somewhere deep in the forest is the occult plant, still undiscovered, which the Soviets thought could cure pustules and poxes. If used correctly, they believed it could revive the grid, permanently rid it of any future breakdowns and spontaneous tragedies. When applied to the temple wall, it was said, the plant would carry the resonance of the bells to the underworld. The plant, as it was imagined by its seekers, was often regarded as being without, or outside of, nature. Even though it was embedded in the forest ecology, which is where all the search for it was primarily conducted, the only way the plant could effect its powers was by being at the thresholds of both Linnaean and Euclidian classifications. Yes, it lived deep within nature but only as a tenant. Each dawn dividing the forest in four, the Soviets drove a team through each quadrant. Every plant that could be made divisible was pierced, plugged with metal. Nothing that could render the grid invincible was found. Some have since believed that the plant moves constantly—it changes its place using a singular non-circadian rhythm. Others believe that in fact the plant was never on the forest floor but is submerged inside a dune, where a community of hyenas tend to it. Another theory: there never was a plant, but a seed. Once found and planted, it will render the future lush. The Soviets wanted the plant to imbricate itself in the grid and change the composition of the city. They wanted the plant to act as a neutral event, a weft, that could stall the infinite, save the hand from dusk.

~

i was told to protect the face from noise to drink more water than my
enemies   but the more i consume the less i fight   for mere awareness is
operant   i was told to protect the line from noise   to draw a code around
the proper moon   as it rises over the work site   blighting hours   that still
belong to the night   i arrange a grid that licks the calf into shape   behind
the factory shed   lifts the shahtoot tree fallen in the canal   a grid gagged
with rice in the harvest season   i was told to protect the process from
noise   to write for a reader yet to come   take apart maps that repeat the
instance of leaving   all leaving haunted by leaving raipur   besieged by
her arms   i was told to protect the fold from noise

The face of the angel is itself not historic. It is turned towards the grazing grounds, towards the molten steel, so you can barely see it. The face of the angel registers the grid, even though it is inhibited from reacting to it directly. Each time a new square is added, its face is flooded with light. It is becoming increasingly impossible for the angel to continue hovering over the grid, for there is no halation in exteriority. Without the face the city is still the city. Without the face, however, the mountain no longer the mountain—it is surface. When encountering face of the other within it, the grid can barely contain its scorn. The angel knows that it was invented not for deliverance but apparitions.

History of angels is such that the severely aged painter, who was neglected for the last sixty years since he finished painting the face of the deity, has been invited back today to the special Thursday court of the sovereign, where he would be held accountable, the painter is almost certain, and persecuted for a crime that he has painstakingly executed since the day the mural was finished with much fanfare among the Jain devotees of the town, many of whom were instantly transfixed by the face of the deity sitting at the very centre of the mural, cross-legged butt-naked atop an unfurling lotus with a traditional halo that marks all enlightened subjects in Jain cosmology, with a few thousand angel-hands stretching from the apex of the mural inviting this Tirthankara into heaven and a few hundred clueless heads of the believers rising in front of the Tirthankara still obsessing over his earthly realm, and on the day the temple was inaugurated these hundreds of painted devotees were joined by a few thousands in flesh, who, along with the sovereign, collectively gazed at the exalted face, which was painted with the intention of making it the centre of the known world, a face they had previously imagined, prayed to, even meditated upon in different shapes and forms, and it achieved this aim by becoming a face so bewitchingly austere that every devotee who saw it trembled at their own material attachments, and soon enough there were people flocking to Nagpura from all directions, queuing noisily on the temple staircase and courtyard, queueing in forecourt around the temple neglecting the other twenty-four deities who, as is customary in Jain temples across the subcontinent, were placed under elongated domes, and arranged in a square layout with each cardinal direction leading to one of them, but it was only the new mural that drew the hoards, who were eager to confirm all rumours of being rendered helpless in encountering the face, something confirmed by the sovereign himself through his unassailable morning routine of crossing the finely carved columns of the temple, and standing quietly in front of the face that made him shiver and powerless for a few seconds every day, a feeling not long or powerful enough to make him want to renunciate his physical pleasures or sovereign powers as was the way of the divine Tirthankaras, something the painter knew all too well, that neither the sovereign nor the Jain devotees who frequented the temple, were going to be moved by the face to an extent that they would relinquish the world and embrace the enlightened path, all the same it was the very austerity of the face that pulled them towards the mural, a crass irony that made life unbearable for the painter, as he felt personally responsible for giving birth to this vulgar contradiction, for taking on a commission to paint the Tirthankara in all his sparseness, for an audience steeped in excess, and to think that he no inkling of what awaited this face for all the three years he laboured over it, traveling several parts of the subcontinent to see other depictions of the Tirthankara's face in ancient Jain manuscripts, temple columns, privately-owned sculptures, and the dissatisfaction that followed these visits, which made him start frequenting Jain monasteries in different regions, sketching the monks he met there, especially monks who were emaciated from observing bodily penance and ritualistic fasting for years, and from time to time he also accompanied the royal stationer to the far reaches of the kingdom to extract the correct kinds of grasses, fruits, urines, and grains from which the pigment for the face could be derived, but nothing prepared him for the actual work of drawing the face, with a raw piece of chalk on a cold grey sandstone, the very sandstone that made up the hill upon which the temple stood, but once the spot for the mural was selected it was that empty patch of sandstone flanked by paint on either side that pierced the painter's dreams, empty against the vast reserve of sandstone that lay intricately chiselled and painted around him, and remained dense yet unformed under him, inside the mountain, but it was only this small empty patch of sandstone that concerned him, and he saw to it that each evening this patch was coated in a cowdung cast protecting the surface from any erosion until the crack of dawn, which is until the cast would be broken and he would start sketching the face once again, a task that took him almost six months to finish, the primary outline of the jaw, the drooping eyes, the nose, the tonsured head, and an equanimous smile that betrayed nothing about the person wearing it, and once this sketch was ready the hard toil of finding the right colour tone for every inch of the face overtook the painter's days, as he mixed colours well aware that the gradient he had achieved for the nostrils, the temples, or the lower zygoma, was nowhere close to the colour that had overwhelmed him in a twelfth century Jain manuscript he had found in a merchant's house in Meerut, nor did the shape of the eyelids or the pupils possess the grace that had moved him deeply in a Tirthankara statue he had found in an abandoned cave near Palitana, but he did not let these doubts stall the process of finding the one true face for the Tirthankara, however different or underwhelming the face might be in comparison to the face that he held in secret, in his mind's eye, where the face had achieved complete perfection and did not belong to a world touched by humanity, and knowing this face secretly was enough of a reward for the painter to not air his doubts publicly or around his apprentices, who saw him slowly finish painting the face over the course of three years, assisting him with the mixing of pigment, finding the right hue and intensity of the colour, the correct angle of the shadow, and throughout this process they did not once suspect the painter of being anything less than enthusiastic about the mural, nor did the sovereign, who urged him to demand an appropriate reward for his services to the State and to the ancient temple premises, and the painter's reply, as was clear to all its witnesses, was well calculated, perhaps articulated well before the sovereign's arrival, and so quick was this demand that no one noticed its eccentricity: the painter was to be allowed to come and pay homage to the face of the Tirthankara, to the mural he had painted, alone and in complete silence, every morning until his death, a demand that the sovereign accepted grudgingly knowing well that the first view of a deity's face was customarily reserved for a sovereign's eye, and it was may be this realisation that made the sovereign grant only the twenty minutes in total to the painter for his every visit, a restriction that barely fazed the painter who was content to have secured any time at all with the mural alone, a mural that he despised exceedingly ever since he finished the painting the face, the proportions and contours of which could not even remotely summon the moment of awakening, the singular gaze, the trance-like calm of the Tirthankara, the face that could renounce everyone and everything, his own body, in the pursuit of absolute non-violence, yet the face in the mural remained a human face, ripe with human desires for kindness, grace, and recognition, it could not simply be forgotten and lost in the mural, it invited attention, demanded admiration, a crime that could have been avoided if only the mural was never commissioned, the painter was never urged to paint a face, this face among all others, which should have been left unformed, yet-to-come, invisible, never forced into appearance, at least not by him, who was now alone with the onerous guilt of depicting the great Tirthankara with a beautiful face that could have been passed off as any ordinary human face—a biological fact made possible by one's mere birth—but the Tirthankara's face, everyone agreed, was something one attains over time, after arduous penance and knowledge of a singular reality around oneself, hence the painter hated that the sovereign and every visitor who set their eyes on this inadequate face mistook it for divinity, their gazes sunk the painter further in his misery and making him work with even more ardour on his plans to deface the mural, to temper the force of his failure, to somehow make the deity invisible again, to hide the Tirthankara from the gaze of the onlookers who consumed the face as they would consume any ordinary object, extraordinary delight followed by indifference, and this tepid aftermath was enough to trigger the painter's sixty years long task within the inner sanctum of temple, undertaken every day at dawn, unaccompanied and before the pujaris got there, with a single piece of white satin cloth tied around his waist, falling all the way to his ankles, and the same cloth rising over his left shoulder, making an oval shaped ring across his chest and shoulder blades before being tucked back into the tight fold of cloth around his waist, his hands hung limply from their joints as he climbed over three hundred steps to cross the first threshold into the temple-city and took small steps across the octagonal courtyard toward the mural, the cold marbled floor hurting his dry, chapped feet, much more painful though was the pointed wooden end of paintbrush that he had carefully concealed in the cloth around his chest along with small jar of freshly mixed paint, and despite the many risks of his undertaking, the journey to the mural every morning was deeply calming for the painter, he saw the twenty-four domes of the temple-city stretched out into the sky pleading for more light, the air inside the temple walls still thick from all the incense burnt a day before, he saw the stillness of the morning, unlived until now, broken only by the evening's debris—pieces of torn cloth, nests of hair, lost earrings—and due to the overbearing arches around him the mural did not become visiting until he was right in front it, where he unsheathed the carefully hidden brush, painting over one of the many smaller faces in mural, faces that surrounded the one true face, and this, this work of revision, of vandalism, in the painter's mind, was carried out in a unison, without losing more than a single breath, as he persisted with this sequence on his every visit, leisurely painting over faces that had already been painted, with the goal to finish retouching every face in the mural except the Tirthankar's, totalling to some three thousand faces among three thousand and one faces, and in making such minute changes spread evenly across six decades he hoped that by the end no one would notice how every face in the mural, including the Tirthankar's, was starting to appear exactly alike, displacing the deity in his own mural, as was obvious to the painter the Tirthankar's face could not be tinkered with, or hidden behind a branch, or a falling leaf, the only way to make him invisible in its own mural would be to make it radically synonymous, alike every face surrounding it, and walking to the court this morning having been summoned for the special assembly by the sovereign the painter wondered if someone has finally caught up and noticed that the one true face of deep, after sixty years of its inauguration, the Tirthankar's austere gaze, was now just a motif repeated all over the mural, in this vast surround of sameness the deity had in fact stepped away from the lotus, away from the attendant angels, and definitively retreated behind the Sal trees that lined the horizon of the mural—

The plant

is to be used for

technical aid

estimated

contemplated.

scheduled

the plant

plants

with West German assistance,

have caused

problems

███ are ███ plants ███

███ critical

███

███ of ███ schedule.

III. WITH SUR–

so
let it fall my
blemishes
slip   away
unclasped
between
this   body
running
oil
horn
in the power
plant
arrow
in the evening
azaan
cleave
to the attention
of red kites
lolling
above
the mahua
unaware
of the tree's
past
don't they say
your name—
hari means
single-glazed
windows
trickle vented
forgiving late
capital again
& hands
digging
infra-
systems
loyalists
team

players
all minutely
remotely
peer reviewed
pull me
by my wrist
hari
ferry me
in
and then out
of this world
lumping iron
in the square
pedestal
in the faint
hearted
a pointillist face
bending neck
lips split
a saffron
welded grid
tight bosom
sharp
but faceless
essence
of ductility
felt on the
goat's neck
in daryaganj
iron tethered
to the butcher
hands
metal's
inner life
without
interiority
for paras stone

all iron
is already
gold
butcher's tool
or   a god
in the making
cloudy river
leaves dev-
prayaag
twisting
the stones
of benares
leaving grass
between
their teeth
the river
gets entombed
in the same ocean
as that gutter
out of
lower howrah
where marwari
ancestors
toss loose
cotton yarn
insured life
pleads
your expanding
soul hari
carry me
with you
beyond this
world border
slow visa
to your breath
a centrally
heated

house
in your voice
ever waiting
to burst
into a soft
joyous
tension
      fish me out
for good
this time
by your mercy
murari
wading through
sludge
the ocean
of this world
illusion embracing
flickering
halogen
moths collecting
over a billboard
selling top-tier
assam tea
first flush
these
are seriously
deep
waters
toe-up greed
sends electric
waves
through
the grid
mollifying
vibrating
matter
in the dull

carcass
of march
light
waves
thudding
over solid
grey
extractions
the ever
fastening
grip   mild
drowning
takes me
further into the
throes of
the marketplace
its rage
a constant lust
and camaraderie
of those friends
of   the grid
who prevent
me from seeing
the lifeboat
with your
name on it:
'murari'
the boat that
could have
pulled a quick one
on these deep
pelagic noises
chimeras
regulate
our sense-complex
they nibble
at me

like fishes in
these waters
my own
follies
deadweight
owing to which
i cannot
find a footing
anywhere
in the end-
less
          lyric
drift
delicate hands
of sea weeds
keep me
exactly
where i am
waters mixing
near the stern
a bullet
an opening
tired without
depletion
living without
life
haven't i
practised
enough of
my gaffes
slips   slippages
to plead your
mercy
shyam   the one
& only
from braj
would you

please
just rescue
me now
picking me
up in
those thick-
veined
        arms
sur has failed
to hold
you
you together
in his
hands
in his
porous
seize
hari
my one
true
non-
transferable
asset
loving you
is never
enough
instead
tell me
why one
loves you
or in
our
sweeping
way   why
one loves
at all
i have

looked
behind every
jamb
to catch
a glimpse
of you
in the alcoves
open pastures
sidewalks
through
every
lattice
protecting
the exhibit
no one
ever
told me
the whole city
was planned
in your image
built to
shelter you
every house
every window
my gaze
their labour
all was you
all one could
think
or run out
of thought
thinking
was you
i have hummed
your name as
simply
'you'

without fail
without
giving you
any other name
without
naming your
traits
form
without
frontiers
without
suburbs
without
the one
true
raipur
wasn't 'hari'
a decoy
a front
for those
that hide
their epistemic
crimes
as have i
hari
a reserve
of mercy
a face
without
facing
would you
not forgive
me
for i have
run amok
with my own
claims

reveries
of being
salvaged
by things
i have touched
to have
repaired
gradually
by those
that are
legible
those that
      are measured
will you
let the beast—
sur's cow—
look you
in the face
hari
tighten the
rope around
its neck
strap it
to the ground
let it taste
the land
for it wanders
around the grid
without
path marks
forever
distorting
my command
inventing
directions
the beast
belongs to

no grid
hari
instead, it has
a stomach
the unfinished
project of
thirst
its mouth
half open
on the motorway
like nothing will
ever complete its
arc
where i
see shelter
it sees the word
yearn
its horns
tear the pages
of law
the eighteen taps
it drinks from
are dry
its desire
is a cavern
with a broken
floor
if you were to
let this beast
lick through
an infinite
catalogue
of tastes
its tongue
would still
await that
one final

impossible
relish
as it flings
itself towards
the world
extracts from
oceans
forests
mountains
it aggressively
forages
heavens
its toes
restlessly needle
the soil
as it walks
attempting to
reach
the very centre
of earth
no world
or word
is enough
everything
in which it
enters
it finds peripheries
the beast
now is on its
fifteenth world
dark hooves
red belly
white horns
like mould
develop
on its head
equipped with

everything it needs
it tempts the world
unafraid of
anything   in our
known world
daemons have
been cut
slayed in half
by its nails
gods have been
tossed between
its horns
a face so deep
it distracts
the grid
many have tried
to tame it
& failed
so hari
tell me
how will
a loser
like me
make it
stick
to its
appointed
pastures
how will i ever
tie it up
near my bed
& let the evening
open its eyes
to blindness
if only
you would
let me

move on
hari
& find
some
other gods
find in
them
true mercy
so—with sur's
transilience
i would
not have to
come back
to you
with the
same prayer
but
each time
i have
gone
away
begging
others—
shiva
brahma
gods and
petty-gods
sages and
wages
reptiles and
relatives
like a debtor
fishing for
new
creditors
knocking
on every

door
i find
maybe
i was
stupid
to have left
your shore
alone
unmoored
in the ocean
falling deeper
in the great
telephonic
scam
of being
awaiting
death
to come
and grab me
like a wolf
grabs
a goat from
behind
i have been
pulled by
my senses
a mad elephant
rollicking
in the mud
mistaking it
for the womb
a tamed monkey
i have moved
in every possible
direction
led by my senses
an owl with a

weak eye
might choose
not to
believe in the sun
but i chose to
sift through
the world's
debris
to see you
there
still out
of reach
listen hari
you have removed
many a trouble
with a pinch
why don't
you take me
into your care
the times
are odd
ghastly with pain
and i could
do with some
finer touches
final repairs
but   sur's suffering
is all-encompassing
direct
forthright
all my love
my capacity
for lush
critical theory
for suffering
in the earth's
shadow

is set aside
for all
that
is not
hari—
lust
rage
ability
birth's
endless
machinery—
like a bee
having
tasted
the one true
nectar
does not
hover
around
the forest
go down
an aisle
shopping
for new
seasonings
it does not
knock
on the mouth
of every
flower
demanding
different
fix
it searches for
the very
thing
a sameness

that does not
exhaust
the bee
a sameness
that moves
in no other
grid
but its own
extracted
from any
other source
it is no
longer the thing
that is how
i wish to
attach myself to
hari
with the single-
mindedness
of the crested
cuckoo
who wakes
with pleas
to the raincloud
& whose songs
have no notes
no lyric
other than
the repetition
of the proper
name:
     'cloud'
a rounded
metonym
for rain
its longing
so singular

all epithets
aerated
sounds
not bearing
the concept
of the cloud
of an over-
whelming
rain
are cast aside
as meaningless
the cuckoo sings
one word
& that alone
is its song
i can pile
more metaphors
for this dangerous
intimacy
that i   crave
with you   hari:
moth & flame
fish & water
everywhere
mediums
that allow
immersion
without fussing
over
the immersed
ways the body
sinks
in the grid
without
offsetting
any urgent
waves   they demand

WHAT CAN SUR GIVE YOU THAT THE GRID CANNOT
WHAT CAN SUR GIVE YOU THAT THE GRID CANNOT
WHAT CAN SUR GIVE YOU THAT THE GRID CANNOT
WHAT CAN SUR GIVE YOU THAT THE GRID CANNOT
WHAT CAN SUR GIVE YOU THAT THE GRID CANNOT
WHAT CAN SUR GIVE YOU THAT THE GRID CANNOT
WHAT CAN SUR GIVE YOU THAT THE GRID CANNOT
WHAT CAN SUR GIVE YOU THAT THE GRID CANNOT
WHAT CAN SUR GIVE YOU THAT THE GRID CANNOT
WHAT CAN SUR GIVE YOU THAT THE GRID CANNOT
WHAT CAN SUR GIVE YOU THAT THE GRID CANNOT
WHAT CAN SUR GIVE YOU THAT THE GRID CANNOT
WHAT CAN SUR GIVE YOU THAT THE GRID CANNOT
WHAT CAN SUR GIVE YOU THAT THE GRID CANNOT
WHAT CAN SUR GIVE YOU THAT THE GRID CANNOT
WHAT CAN SUR GIVE YOU THAT THE GRID CANNOT
WHAT CAN SUR GIVE YOU THAT THE GRID CANNOT
WHAT CAN SUR GIVE YOU THAT THE GRID CANNOT
WHAT CAN SUR GIVE YOU THAT THE GRID CANNOT
WHAT CAN SUR GIVE YOU THAT THE GRID CANNOT
WHAT CAN SUR GIVE YOU THAT THE GRID CANNOT
WHAT CAN SUR GIVE YOU THAT THE GRID CANNOT
WHAT CAN SUR GIVE YOU THAT THE GRID CANNOT
WHAT CAN SUR GIVE YOU THAT THE GRID CANNOT
WHAT CAN SUR GIVE YOU THAT THE GRID CANNOT
WHAT CAN SUR GIVE YOU THAT THE GRID CANNOT
WHAT CAN SUR GIVE YOU THAT THE GRID CANNOT
WHAT CAN SUR GIVE YOU THAT THE GRID CANNOT
WHAT CAN SUR GIVE YOU THAT THE GRID CANNOT
WHAT CAN SUR GIVE YOU THAT THE GRID CANNOT
WHAT CAN SUR GIVE YOU THAT THE GRID CANNOT
WHAT CAN SUR GIVE YOU THAT THE GRID CANNOT
WHAT CAN SUR GIVE YOU THAT THE GRID CANNOT
WHAT CAN SUR GIVE YOU THAT THE GRID CANNOT
WHAT CAN SUR GIVE YOU THAT THE GRID CANNOT
WHAT CAN SUR GIVE YOU THAT THE GRID CANNOT
WHAT CAN SUR GIVE YOU THAT THE GRID CANNOT
WHAT CAN SUR GIVE YOU THAT THE GRID CANNOT

let my passion
sink
its teeth
silently
in your
flesh
hari
where it
will remain
lodged
forgetting
all other
names
in seeking
carrying
your
love hari
in the well
of my eyes
my hands
i will suffer
in this stillness
stop
drifting
stop loving
again
no longer
in the world
suffer
in sameness
& find there
a lewd fire
a shelter
that could
burn
this life
to some indivisible

residue
to a stone
that has
never
not known
semblance
sur's home
is drained
of ideas
it is
open to
visitors
but no one
lingers
longer than a
second
the house
thinks too
hard about
mortgage
its internal
decorum
too little
about termites
sur's home
was built
above the ruins
of your
lotus-feet
hari
finding once
an alcove
in your feet
between your
calluses
sur had not
needed a home

but now
he has one
& he is hard
at work
like a dog
ceaselessly
rambling
licking clean
pots in
other people's
houses
sur is now
both surplus
& waste
his home
feeds on
funeral pyres
where limit
births
desire
the home
is driven
by growth
lifts its roof
applies for a
permit
to raise another
floor
in its
cancerous
growth
the house
remains
legible
to those
that surround it
even as it

thrives
sur's home
shrinks
inside the
house
wherever
it looks
outside itself
it shudders in
fear
its sea-facing
windows
are clogged
with seagull
nests
its valley view
blocked
by a youth
hostel
a wind
turbine
cuts
through
its sunsets
sur drifts
to other houses
other shelter
each more
inadequate
than the last
hari
you who
shelters
the world
will you
check in
sur

the fool he is
always
pays
up front
for a floor
plan
only to be
lost
        again
spare me
the blushes
hari
you already
know all
there is
to know
i am not
my play
list
nor my
soft
deposits
over
the years
i have let
my failings
blunders
misreadings
make a nest
inside me
all petty
tiresome
errors
like twigs
both receive
and sever
us two

leaving
you as plural
inside me
even as
time passes
illusions thrive
around me
i soak myself
in all that is
carnal
filial
sartorial
libidinal
anecdotal
language
traps me
sentience
buries me further
somewhere
in the engine
of this boat
that refuses
to budge
to take me
across
away
from here
        where
everything is
the world
& not
the future
even though
i keep saying
to the boatmen:
'this is not
the world'

lift me from
this shallow end
from this
airtight grid
hari
spot me
in the cross hairs
hari
during the
cosmic splurge
when all
that is far
moves
under
one skin
a common
unperturbed
texture
that is how
far
& close
i have held
this apology
let my shame
be yours
always yours
hari
take it
take me
with you
into new
timeliness
an imploding
prosody
    a new
new
    delay—

██ the plant is ██████████

ceeding satisfactorily.

The redacted extracts on 'the plant' are from the CIA report titled 'USSR Assistance for the Bhilai Steel Plant in India'. It was approved for public release on 2000/09/11 and is classed as a secret file under the reference number, CIA-RDP62S00545A000100090098-0.

The long poem 'With Sur' is a reworking and remixing of medieval hymns attributed to the saint-poet Surdas and originally written in Braj.

Previous versions of some of the poems in this collection have appeared in *SpamZine, Datableed, LuddGang, the Hythe, South Parade, Hotel*, and *Almost Island*. My utmost thanks to the editors and readers at these outlets for their enthusiasm for the work.

Thanks to all the early readers and friends of the book.